GOD'S PLAN
A Children's Guide to Jesus As Our Great Salvation in the Bible
Copyright © 2018 by Gerry Escalante
Illustrations by Gerry Escalante

Published by Lucid Books in Houston, TX.
www.LucidBooksPublishing.com

All rights reserved. No part of this publication may be reproduced, stored in a retrieval system, or transmitted in any form by any means, electronic, mechanical, photocopy, recording, or otherwise, without the prior permission of the publisher, except as provided for by USA copyright law.

ISBN-10: 1-63296-221-7
ISBN-13: 978-1-63296-221-8
eISBN-10: 1-63296-220-9
eISBN-13: 978-1-63296-220-1

Special Sales: Most Lucid Books titles are available in special quantity discounts. Custom imprinting or excerpting can also be done to fit special needs. Contact Lucid Books at info@lucidbookspublishing.com.

Kari, I thank you for being a supportive and imaginative wife through all of this.

Nayomi, Eva, and Sayla, thank you for keeping Dadda thinking of Jesus as the super big hero that He is.

In the beginning, *God* created
everything you see:
planets, mountains, animals,
and every kind of tree.

God created man
and woman in His likeness
and placed them in a garden
to reflect His brightness.

Adam and his wife Eve
were the first people.
They talked and walked with *God*
in a union that was peaceful.

God offered to them
to eat freely of any tree,
except from the tree of good and evil.
"Okay!" they said. "We agree!"

But then a serpent came to trick them
when the sky was blue,
hissing "*God* is hiding something
so special from you."

"Look at this fruit
juicy, ripe, and sweet.
Why wouldn't *God*
give you this to eat?"

Eve and Adam ate the fruit,
and this filled their hearts with sadness.

Now, sin and death would spread
to all who bore *God's* likeness.
Oh no!
Yet this part is important
in *God's* awesome story.
Men and women would now
be separated from *God's* glory.

The story is not yet done;
there is more to share:
God's plan would not fail
not here nor there.

God's plan to restore peace
with His people had begun;
He'd always planned to send
His one and only Son.

Now, more and more people
were filling up the land.
Evil thoughts were in the hearts
of every child, woman, and man.

"My plan is to discipline these people,"
God said unhappily.
He told a man named Noah,
"Build a boat for you and all your family."

"Bring a pair of every kind
of animal you see:
Furry, fuzzy, and scaly
from the greatest to the least."

For forty nights, rain poured down
and then suddenly stopped.
After many wet and stormy days,
the giant boat had docked.

God made a promise
by making a rainbow appear—
to never flood the earth with water
and still bring His people near.

To become a friend of *God*,
no one would need a boat,
for *God* planned to send His Son
to make this promise forever float.

Time marched forward
and so did *God* our Rock
to seek that union with His people, like a
shepherd and his flock.

As a part of the great plan,
God called not a mighty man
but a common man.

In the night, *God* told Abraham
to look up into the sky,
"More children than these stars,
through your family shall arrive."

God proclaimed in heaven,
"I'm happy with Abraham
for trusting my promise
and believing in My perfect plan."

God kept His promise;
Abraham's wife bore a son.
They praised *God* for baby Isaac,
but *God's* plan to bring us back was not quite done.

Years later, *God* asked Abraham
to make a sacrifice.
(A sacrifice means giving up
something of great price.)

So, He said, "Take your son, your lovely
one up the mountain to give to me."
Abraham obeyed the Lord
and said, "So shall it be!"

While Abraham and Isaac walked,
Isaac looked confused.
He saw some wood to burn,
but where's the lamb to use?

Isaac knew *God* required
a lamb to be given—
not frogs, snails, or quails.
Not a hairy pig and not a chicken.

"My son, our *God* Himself
will provide the right One,"
Abraham assured
his precious puzzled son.

God did provide a sacrifice, but it was not a lamb.
It was a long-horned animal.

Can you guess?

Yes! A ram.
The Lamb of God would come later
in the form of a man.

Abraham rejoiced! His son was saved,
and there is more to share:
God's plan would not fail.
Not here nor there nor anywhere.

God would give His own Son, His lovely One,
for those who believe to restore the peaceful
union God once shared with
Adam and Eve!

God's plan like a flower
continued to unfold.
Do not forget that dwelling with us
was His ultimate goal.

Abraham and Sarah's family
grew and grew more.
Where they lived, there was no food,
but Egypt had food galore.

In Egypt as the "Sons of Israel,"
the family became known.
The Egyptians were afraid of them,
for in numbers they had grown.

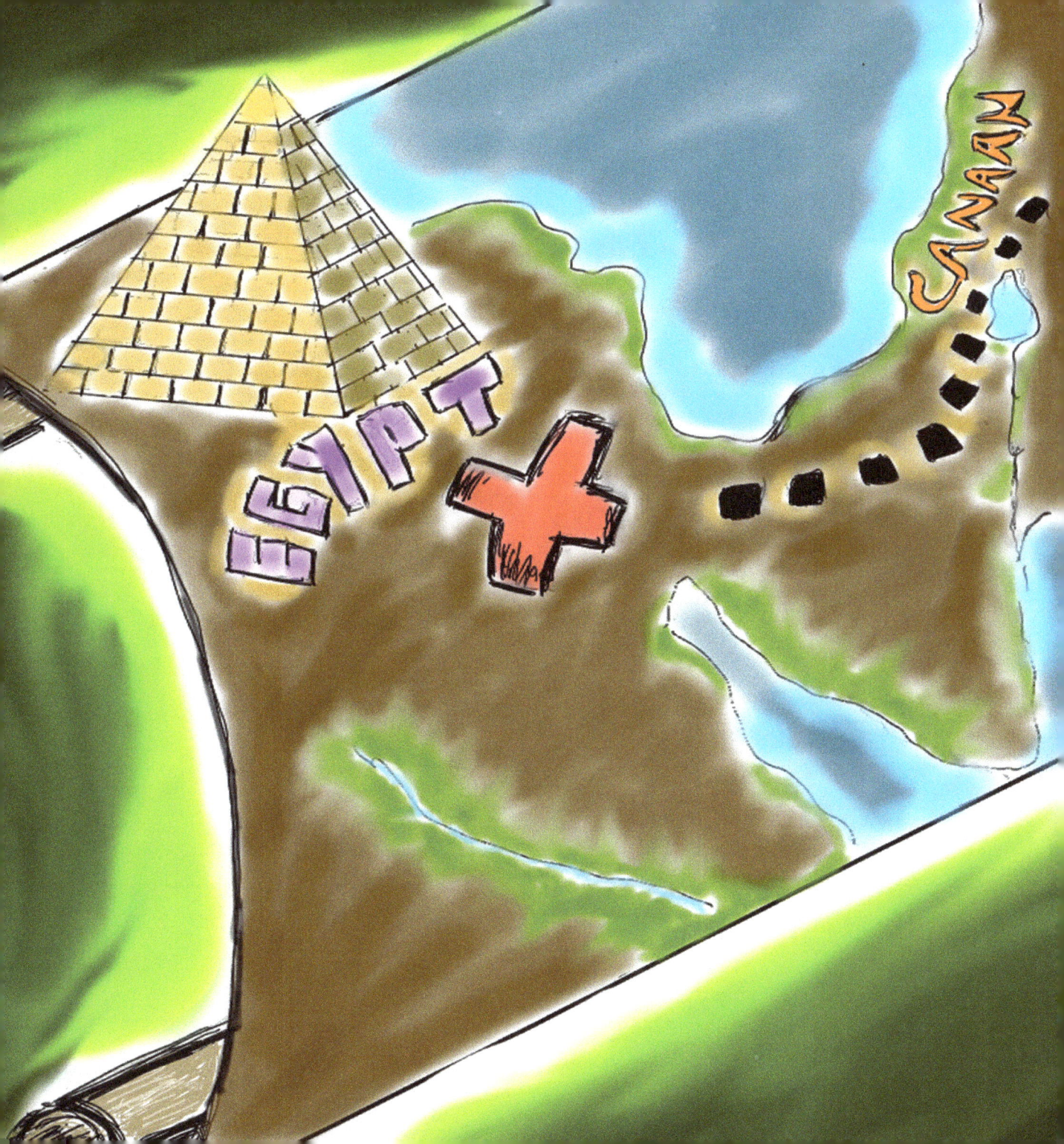

Ruling over the land,
Pharaoh also had a plan
to stop the Sons of Israel
from taking over the land.

Pharaoh plotted to get rid
of every Israelite male baby.
So, a mother hid her son
and made a plan for his safety.

She placed the boy in blankets
in a basket made of reeds
and sent him swooshing down a river
for a chance to live free.

Pharaoh's daughter found the basket
and named the baby Moses.
God's people became Egypt's slaves.
Now, things were looking hopeless.

God called to Moses
through a burning bush.
"Moses! To Pharaoh I will send you.
His armies I will crush."

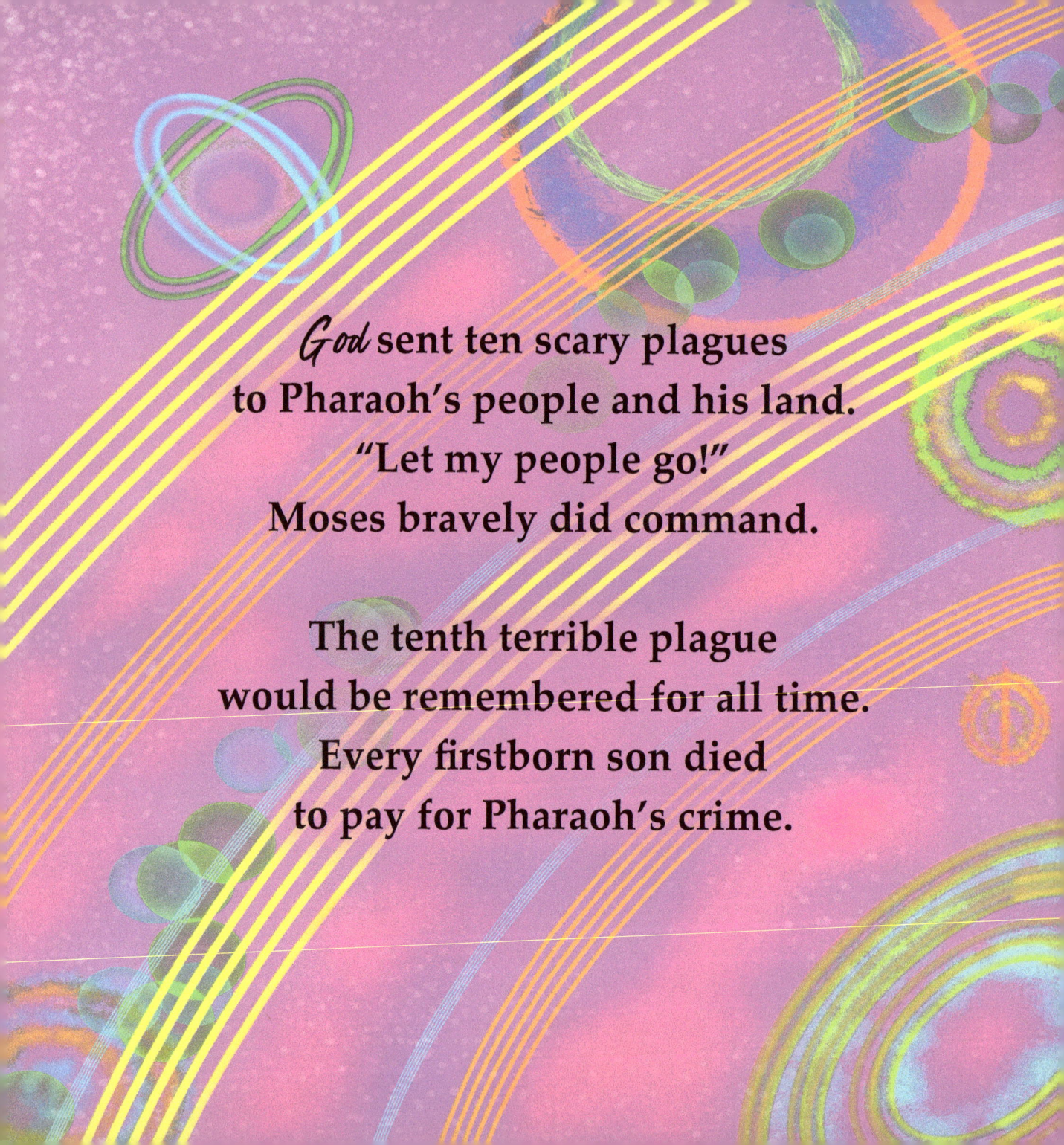

God sent ten scary plagues
to Pharaoh's people and his land.
"Let my people go!"
Moses bravely did command.

The tenth terrible plague
would be remembered for all time.
Every firstborn son died
to pay for Pharaoh's crime.

Yet, *God* spared those
who obeyed this command:
"Spread above your doorposts
the blood of a spotless lamb."

The Israelites would celebrate
this night for years to come.
God was planning something more
that never had been done.

There would come a day
God would save us from slavery.
Not from chains or awful kings
but from sin's captivity.

The freed people left Egypt
and walked into the wilderness.
They soon missed their homes
and grumbled with much bitterness.

Yet, *God* provided for their needs
with shade and bread to eat.
Leading them by night with fire
and providing water—what a treat!

Throughout the years, *God* sent His people
prophets, priests, and kings
to reunite their hearts with Him,
the King who is their everything.

But their relationship felt broken,
and the Israelites praised false idols.
God was mightily displeased,
for He would have no other rivals.

The Israelites were troubled
as was to be expected.
God did not speak.
Israel seemed rejected.

Until one glorious night—
Angels shouted as they swooped down:
"A baby is born who is worthy
of an everlasting crown."

A celebration had begun.
Lowly shepherds were invited.
With joy, wise men from afar
by a star were guided.

What they found was great—
a child who is *God* in human skin,
the Creator who holds the heavens
and can be our greatest friend.

JESUS!

Yes! His name means "*God* will save
His people from their sin."
He was born in a barn,
for there was no room in the inn.

There are many stories to tell about *Jesus*,
but time would certainly fail.
God's plan to bring us close to Him
would first have to rip the veil.

For remember at the beginning
of *God's* amazing story,
we were all separated
far away from His glory.

Now, the moment all creation
had waited for was here.
Jesus would be sacrificed
to bring His people near.

He died and was buried,
but didn't stay that way.
On the third day, *Jesus* arose!
He conquered the grave!

He told his friends,
"I was always *God's* plan.
There is now forgiveness of sin
for any child, woman, and man."

"I will come back,
for this is *God's* heart:
to bring His children close
and never be apart."

Now, we wait with eagerness for that amazing
day when we will see Him face-to-face—
"O Lord, please come, we pray!"

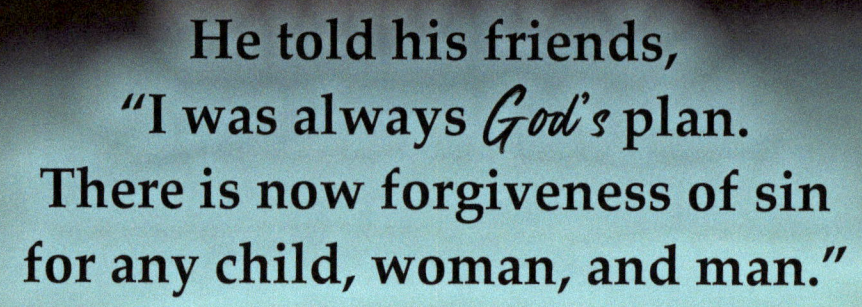

Digging Deeper with Your Children

1. Abraham was willing to give up his son to God. God did give up His son for you. What item do you have that would be difficult for you to give up if God asked you to give it to Him?

2. God sent Moses to free His people from Pharaoh. Jesus was sent by God to free us from sin. What sin do you need Jesus to free you from?

3. God's relationship with Israel was broken because they served idols. So, when God stopped talking to them, they must have felt alone and maybe sad. When you feel sad or lonely because you have done something wrong, how do you know that God still loves you?

4. What was God's plan to bring back His lost people to Him?

5. Jesus is God's great plan of salvation. Jesus tells His disciples to tell everyone about Him. Who do you know who needs to hear about Jesus? Pray to Jesus that they will come to know Him.

ABOUT THE AUTHOR

Gerry Escalante lives in California's High Desert with his wife, Kari, and their three daughters. He is a Worship Leader and Elder at Oasis Community Church in Hesperia, California. Born and raised in Los Angeles, Gerry became a Christian while attending California State University in Los Angeles to pursue his degree in Child Development. When Gerry later began teaching his daughters about the Bible and how all its stories point to God's plan of salvation through Jesus, he desired a fun, entertaining picture book that would portray these rich truths of God's awesome story. Because of his love for drawing and Scripture study, Gerry then set out to create his own book. It is Gerry's hope that this story will help other families with young children see God's master plan of salvation unfold.

www.ingramcontent.com/pod-product-compliance
Lightning Source LLC
LaVergne TN
LVHW070948070426
835507LV00028B/3453